I HAVE MONSTERS IN MY TUMMY

Proofreading
Carolina Casarin
Guilherme Semionato

Art
Relâmpago

Photography
Bruno Alvares

- @toniacasarin | @meusmonstrinhos
- @toniacasarin | @tenhomonstrosnabarriga
- Tenho Monstros na Barriga

perfil.toniacasarin.com.br/en-us/

I HAVE MONSTERS IN MY TUMMY

TONIA CASARIN

2nd edition

2019

To Felipe, Ieiê, Fernandinho and Marcos.
To Tuca, Thi and Lua.
To the kid that lives within me.
And to the one who lives in Carlos.

This is the story of Marcelo, a boy who is always feeling a lot of things in his belly.

"Mommy, there is something in my tummy!"

His mom always says,
"You must be hungry. Or maybe you want to go to the toilet."

He tries everything: going to the toilet, eating a banana – his favorite fruit –, but nothing happens!

Marcelo asks himself,
"What do I have in my tummy that not even my mommy can tell?"

One day, coming home from school, he says to his mom,
"Mommy! Mommy! Today I scored a goal at school!"

Jumping up and down, he says,
"Uh-oh! I'm feeling something in my tummy again…"

His mother explains,
"This thing that you are feeling in your tummy has a name."

But what is Marcelo feeling in his tummy?

Finally, Marcelo understands there are feelings in his tummy.
And he decides to call these feelings his little monsters.
Each feeling is a different monster.

Let's meet Marcelo's little monsters?

One of them comes up when he scores a goal playing soccer or when he plays with his dad all day long in the park.

It is JOY.

Marcelo gets very excited, jumps up and down and cannot stop smiling when he is JOYFUL.

He also notices that when he is JOYFUL, his mom and dad feel the same, because they have a big smile on their faces.

This is the little monster of JOY.

My little monster of JOY appears when:

I remind of a JOYFUL moment that was:

How does my body feel when I am JOYFUL:

I know someone is JOYFUL when:

When the little monster of JOY appears, I know I am JOYFUL.

Draw your little monster of JOY:

One day, at recess, Marcelo got hurt. That was the day when he met another little monster.

It was SADNESS.

This little monster also came up when his best friend did not let him play with a toy. Marcelo noticed that when the little monster of SAD appears, he does not want to talk and has a huuuuuuuuge need to cry. It is because he is SAD.

When he is SAD his shoulders get heavy, he looks down and has a big frown, like a frog.

This is the little monster of SADNESS.

My little monster of SADNESS appears when:

I remind of a SAD moment that was:

How does my body feel when I am SAD:

I know someone is SAD when:

When the little monster of SADNESS appears, I know I am SAD.

Draw your little monster of SADNESS:

Sometimes Marcelo feels a very agitated monster coming to life in his belly, especially when his sister changes the TV channel he is watching.

He also feels ANGRY when he wants to tell about his day at school, and no one listens.

He noticed that when he is ANGRY he wants to scream and show everyone how strong he is.

When people are ANGRY, they usually bite their lips and make a scary face.

This is the little monster of ANGER.

My little monster of ANGER appears when:

I remind of an ANGRY moment that was:

How does my body feel when I am ANGRY:

I know someone is ANGRY when:

When the little monster of ANGER appears, I know I am ANGRY.

Draw your little monster of ANGER:

On a Sunday, Marcelo tried to learn how to ride a skateboard. But the skateboard was too fast!

The little monster of FEAR showed up in his tummy.

This little monster also came when Marcelo was on the beach and wanted to go into the sea, but there were a lot of big waves. They were huuuuuuuge!

Marcelo noticed that when he is AFRAID he thinks about bad things that can happen.

He also noticed that when people are AFRAID, they usually stop trying to learn new things and they freeze, like a statue.

This is the little monster of FEAR.

My little monster of FEAR appears when:

I remind of a moment of FEAR that was:

How does my body feel when I am AFRAID:

I know someone is AFRAID when:

When the little monster of FEAR appears, I know I am AFRAID.

Draw your little monster of FEAR:

At school, Marcelo decided to raise his hand and answer to a question, even though he did not know if it was right.

He felt a big monster taking over his tummy.
He unraveled the mystery.

It was COURAGE.

He realized that COURAGE usually shows up along with FEAR.
"Wow! There is space for more than one monster in my tummy at the same time!"

He remembered another moment when he felt BRAVE. It was when he decided to go into the sea despite all the big waves. He noticed that when he was BRAVE, it was like having superpowers and beating FEAR.

When this happens, he knows nothing can go wrong. When people are BRAVE, they puff out their chest and face FEAR.

This is my little monster of COURAGE.

My little monster of COURAGE appears when:

I remind of a BRAVE moment that was:

How does my body feel when I am feeling BRAVE:

I know someone is feeling BRAVE when:

When the little monster of COURAGE appears, I know I am feeling BRAVE.

Draw your little monster of COURAGE:

When Marcelo went to the zoo with is family during spring break, he was eager to see all the animals.

He refused to go home until he had seen them all.

He discovered that the little monster of CURIOSITY lived in his belly.

He wanted to know why the giraffe had such a long neck, if the zebra and the horse were from the same family, and how the monkeys could jump so high!

The monster of CURIOSITY also showed up when Marcelo wanted to know where ants live. Or how the rain falls from the sky. Or why is pee yellow.

He learned that the little monster of CURIOSITY never stops asking. And even before it knows the answer, it is already asking something else. Even grown-ups don't have all the answers!

This is the little monster of CURIOSITY.

My little monster of CURIOSITY appears when:

I remind of a moment of CURIOSITY that was:

How does my body feel when I am CURIOUS:

I know someone is CURIOUS when:

When the little monster of CURIOSITY appears, I know I am CURIOUS.

Draw your little monster of CURIOSITY:

When Marcelo got a good grade at school, he wanted to show it to his parents right away.

He discovered the little monster of PRIDE in his belly.

He knew how hard he worked to get that grade.

The little monster of PRIDE also showed up when he finished a difficult puzzle. It was like he wanted to praise himself.

When we are PROUD, we remember that if we work hard, we can solve even the hardest puzzles!

This is the little monster of PRIDE.

My little monster of PRIDE appears when:

I remind of a moment of PRIDE that was:

How does my body feel when I am feeling PROUD:

I know someone is feeling PROUD when:

When the little monster of PRIDE appears, I know I am feeling PROUD.

Draw your little monster of PRIDE:

When his little sister was born, a new monster grew in Marcelo's tummy.

It was the little monster of JEALOUSY.

This monster showed up when people wouldn't stop asking about his little sister. It felt as if they liked her better.

He also gets JEALOUS when his best friend pays more attention to other kids.

When he gets JEALOUS, he wants everyone only to himself.

This is the little monster of JEALOUSY.

My little monster of JEALOUSY appears when:

I remind of a moment of JEALOUSY that was:

How does my body feel when I am JEALOUS:

I know someone is JEALOUS when:

When the little monster of JEALOUSY appears, I know I am JEALOUS.

Draw your little monster of JEALOUSY:

Marcelo understands now that many little monsters live inside his tummy. And each one of them shows up in different situations. Sometimes, more than one of them comes up at the same time!

Do you have monsters in your tummy too? And if they live inside your belly anyway, why not become friends with them?

About the author

Tonia Casarin completed her Masters in Education at Teachers College, Columbia University, NY.

She is passionate about children and the emotions that live in all of us. This is her second book. Also by the author: **I Have Monsters in my Tummy.**

@toniacasarin
perfil.toniacasarin.com.br/en-us/

Made in the USA
Lexington, KY
18 September 2019